Pebble® Plus

Cycles of Nature

The Water Cycle

by Catherine Ipcizade

Consultant: Dr. Sandra F. Mather, Professor Emerita
Department of Earth and Space Sciences
West Chester University, West Chester, Pa.

PEBBLE
a capstone imprint

Pebble Plus is published by Pebble
1710 Roe Crest Drive, North Mankato, Minnesota 56003
capstonepub.com

Library of Congress Cataloging-in-Publication Data
Names: Ipcizade, Catherine, author.
Title: The water cycle : a 4D book / by Catherine Ipcizade.
Description: North Mankato, Minnesota : Pebble, [2019] | Series: Pebble plus.
    Cycles of nature | Audience: Ages 4–8.
Identifiers: LCCN 2018002966 (print) | LCCN 2018021552 (ebook) | ISBN
    9781977100474 (eBook PDF) | ISBN 9781977100399 (hardcover) | ISBN
    9781977100436 (pbk.)
Subjects: LCSH: Hydrologic cycle—Juvenile literature. | Rain and
    rainfall—Juvenile literature. | Water—Juvenile literature.
Classification: LCC GB848 (ebook) | LCC GB848 .I63 2019 (print) | DDC
    551.48—dc23
LC record available at https://lccn.loc.gov/2018002966

Summary: Lakes evaporate. Clouds form from condensation. Rain falls and fills rivers and lakes. Soak up facts about the water cycle and why we need to keep water clean.

Editorial Credits
Emily Raij, editor; Charmaine Whitman, designer;
Eric Gohl, media researcher; Kris Wilfahrt, production specialist

Image Credits
Newscom: Blend Images/Ariel Skelley, 21; Shutterstock: aekikuis, 5, Alexey Osokin, cover (left), 1 (left), Eakachai Leesin, 17, FenlioQ, 7, Firstyahoo, cover (bottom), 1 (bottom), Kuzmenko Viktoria, 10, Neirfy, 15, Ostariyanov, 9, pixy_nook, 11, Rich Carey, 19, Serkan Senturk, 13, Zhivka Kalinkova, cover (right), 1 (right)
Design Elements: Shutterstock

Note to Parents and Teachers

The Cycles of Nature set supports the national science standards related to patterns in the natural world. This book describes and illustrates the water cycle. The images support early readers in understanding the text. The repetition of words and phrases helps early readers learn new words. This book also introduces early readers to subject-specific vocabulary words, which are defined in the Glossary section. Early readers may need assistance to read some words and to use the Table of Contents, Glossary, Read More, Internet Sites, Critical Thinking Questions, and Index sections of the book.

Printed in the United States   5961

Table of Contents

The Water Cycle

Grab an umbrella! It's going to rain! A thick cloud moves by. Why does this change in weather happen? It's because of the water cycle!

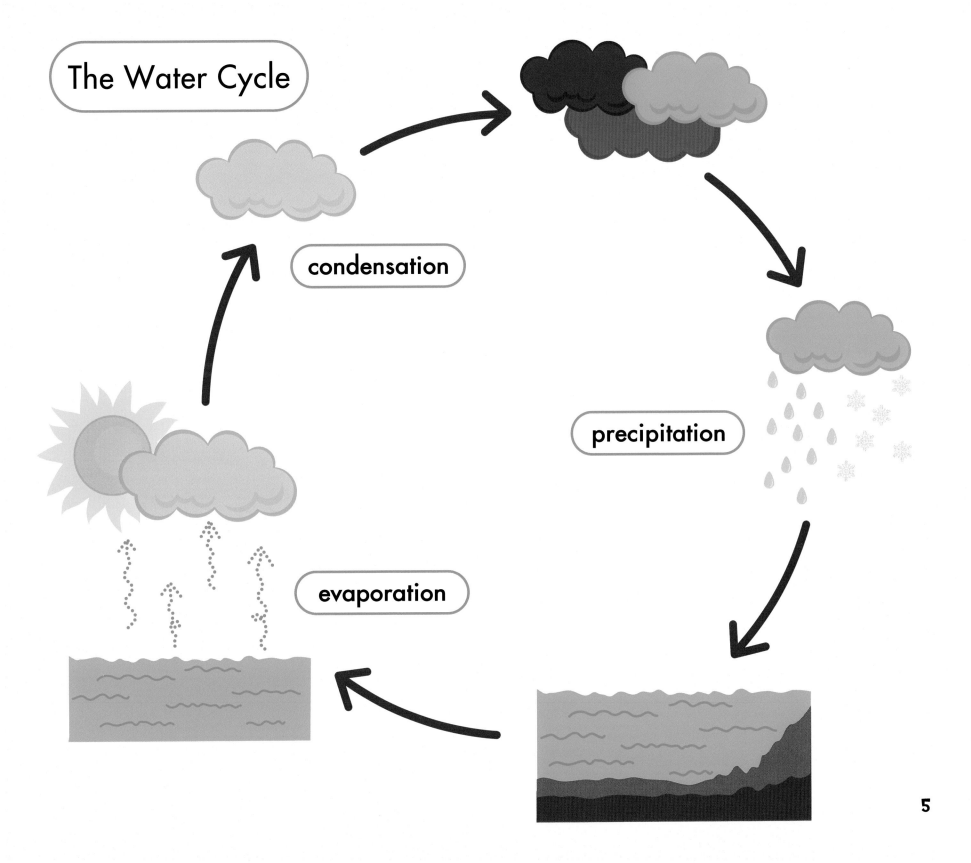

The Water Cycle

condensation

precipitation

evaporation

5

Liquid to Gas

Imagine a lake in summer. Heat from the sun warms the water. Warm water rises in the air and turns into gas.

The gas is vapor.
This process is called
evaporation.
Water evaporates on
plant leaves too.

Clouds at Work

Vapor from lakes and oceans cools. It turns into tiny water droplets. This is called condensation, which makes clouds or dew.

dew

Clouds are made of
water droplets. The droplets
become too heavy. That's when
rain or snow falls. This is
called precipitation.

precipitation

From Water to Ice

Precipitation falls into lakes and oceans. Water can also freeze into ice in cold weather. The water cycle starts again when it gets warm.

People and Water

The water cycle has repeated for billions of years. Our water has been on Earth a long time. We drink the same water the first people on Earth drank!

If we dump chemicals
and trash into the water,
we make water dirty.
This is called pollution.

Dirty water is dangerous
to drink. It can change
what lives and grows in places
too. We need to work to keep
our water clean.

Glossary

condensation—changing from a gas to a liquid

dew—small water droplets that collect overnight on outside surfaces, such as plant leaves

evaporation—changing from a liquid to a gas

pollution—materials that hurt Earth's water, air, and land

precipitation—water that falls from clouds to Earth's surface; precipitation can be rain, hail, sleet, or snow.

vapor—a gas made from a liquid or a solid

weather—the condition outdoors at a certain time and place; weather changes with each season.